NEW YORK STYLE

NEW YORK
Exteriors   Interiors

STYLE
Details

EDITOR **Angelika Taschen**

TASCHEN

HONG KONG KÖLN LONDON LOS ANGELES MADRID PARIS TOKYO

To stay informed about upcoming TASCHEN titles, please request our magazine
at www.taschen.com/magazine or write to TASCHEN, Hohenzollernring 53,
D-50672 Cologne, Germany, contact@taschen.com, Fax: +49-221-254919.
We will be happy to send you a free copy of our magazine which is filled with
information about all of our books.

Edited by Angelika Taschen, Berlin
Layout and project management by Stephanie Bischoff, Cologne
Captions by Christiane Reiter, Berlin
Lithography by Horst Neuzner, Cologne
English translation by Pauline Cumbers, Frankfurt am Main
French translation by Cécile Carrion, Cologne and Philippe Safavi, Paris
German translation by Christiane Burkhardt, Munich

Printed in China
ISBN 978-3-8365-0773-8

CONTENTS SOMMAIRE INHALT

A century or so ago, any conversation about New York style would lead quickly back to the other side of the Atlantic. For until the 20th century, New York's style was an amalgam of European imports, of buildings with "Italianate" facades and interior decorations shipped over by the boatload from Venice and Florence, Brussels and Paris. But in the 20th century, the city of New York changed from an imitator into a global trendsetter. The skyscraper, New York's architectural trademark, transformed Manhattan's skyline, proclaiming that, in the truly modern city, the built environment should be more spectacular than the natural one. Large factories, boasting elaborate facades that made them seem almost like industrial mansions, lined the streets of neighbourhoods busy with manufacturing and shipping. Cosmopolitan, yet quintessentially American in its willingness to break with the humdrum and aim for the sky, New York developed a style glamorous and new, as iconic as the sparkling crown at the top of the Chrysler Building. New York, arguably, is now as settled in its cultural

THE SKY'S THE LIMIT
Daisann McLane

Il y a environ un siècle, toute conversation sur le style new-yor-kais nous ramenait rapidement sur l'autre rive de l'Atlantique. Jusqu'à la fin du 19ᵉ siècle, la ville était un amalgame d'impor-tations européennes, de façades «italianisantes », d'intérieurs décorés de meubles et de bibelots acheminés par cargos entiers depuis Venise, Florence, Bruxelles ou Paris.Puis, au 20ᵉ siècle, la ville est passée d'imitatrice à initiatrice de tendances planétaires. Le gratte-ciel, sa principale caractéristique architec-turale, a transformé la silhouette de Manhattan, proclamant qu'une ville vraiment moderne se devait d'avoir des bâtiments plus spectaculaires que son environnement naturel. Tels des hôtels particuliers industriels, de grandes usines aux façades sophistiquées vinrent border les rues de quartiers spécialisés dans la confection et l'expédition. Cosmopolite mais fondamen-talement américaine dans sa volonté de sortir de la routine et de viser toujours plus haut, New York inventa un nouveau glamour, aussi reconnaissable que la couronne étincelante du Chrysler Building. Aujourd'hui, elle se repose sur ses acquis culturels à l'instar des capitales européennes qu'elle singeait dans son adolescence, mais elle conserve son propre style, en évolution

Vor etwa hundert Jahren hätte eine Unterhaltung zum Thema New Yorker Stil schnell auf die andere Seite des Atlantiks geführt. Bis Anfang des 20. Jhh. war der New Yorker Stil eine Mischung aus europäischer Importware, aus Gebäuden mit italianisierenden Fassaden und Inneneinrichtungen, die man sich mit dem Schiff aus Venedig, Florenz, Brüssel oder Paris kommen ließ. Doch im 20. Jhh. wurde die Stadt New York von der bloßen Nachahmerin zur globalen Trendsetterin. Der Wolkenkratzer, New Yorks archi-tektonisches Wahrzeichen, veränderte die Skyline von Manhattan. Er läutete eine Ära ein, in der die Bauwerke einer modernen Stadt spektakulärer sein müssen als ihre natürliche Umgebung. Große Industriegebäude mit reich verzierten Fassaden, die in ihrer Pracht eher an Herrenhäuser erinnerten, säumten die Straßen, in denen eifrig Waren gehandelt wurden. Das kosmopolitische, aber in seinem Emporstreben typisch amerikanische New York entwi-ckelte einen glamourösen und brandneuen Stil, der bald ebenso zum Kult wurde wie die funkelnde Stahlkrone auf der Spitze des Chrysler Building. Heute ist New York in kultureller Hinsicht genauso etabliert wie die europäischen Hauptstädte, die die junge, aufstrebende Metropole einst imitierte. Ihr Stil ist einzigartig

ways as the European capitals it imitated in its adolescence, yet the city's style remains distinctive, ever-evolving. Leave here for a few months, and when you return, the skyline will be different, the corner grocery will have morphed into an art gallery (and the landlord will have raised your rent!). Space, for decades the gold standard of stylish New York living, is now not enough for New Yorkers. We want room, but it must also have authenticity, bones. We are hooked on architectural detail, on the artefacts of our city's now-lost manufacturing past. Our second great invention, after the skyscraper, is the loft. The industrial "mansions" of fifty years ago are now the coveted high-ceilinged, open-plan spaces of SoHo, of Brooklyn. They are occupied, as New York always has been, by style setters arriving from around the globe, from São Paulo to Shanghai. They move into the all-white, classic pre-war high rise apartment with the view of the Chrysler Building, place a perfect mango-yellow Chinese lamp on the bedside table, and make New York their own, very stylish home.

"...I went up to the top of the Empire State Building. One dollar, twice as expensive as a cinema seat..."

Simone de Beauvoir, in *America Day by Day*

«...Je suis montée au sommet de l'Empire State Building. Un dollar, deux fois plus cher qu'un fauteuil au cinéma...»

Simone de Beauvoir , dans *L'Amérique au jour le jour*

»...Ich bin zur Spitze des Empire State Buildings hinaufgefahren. Ein Dollar, zweimal so teuer wie ein Sperrsitz im Kino...«

Simone de Beauvoir, in *Amerika Tag und Nacht*

EXTERIORS

Extérieurs   Aussichten

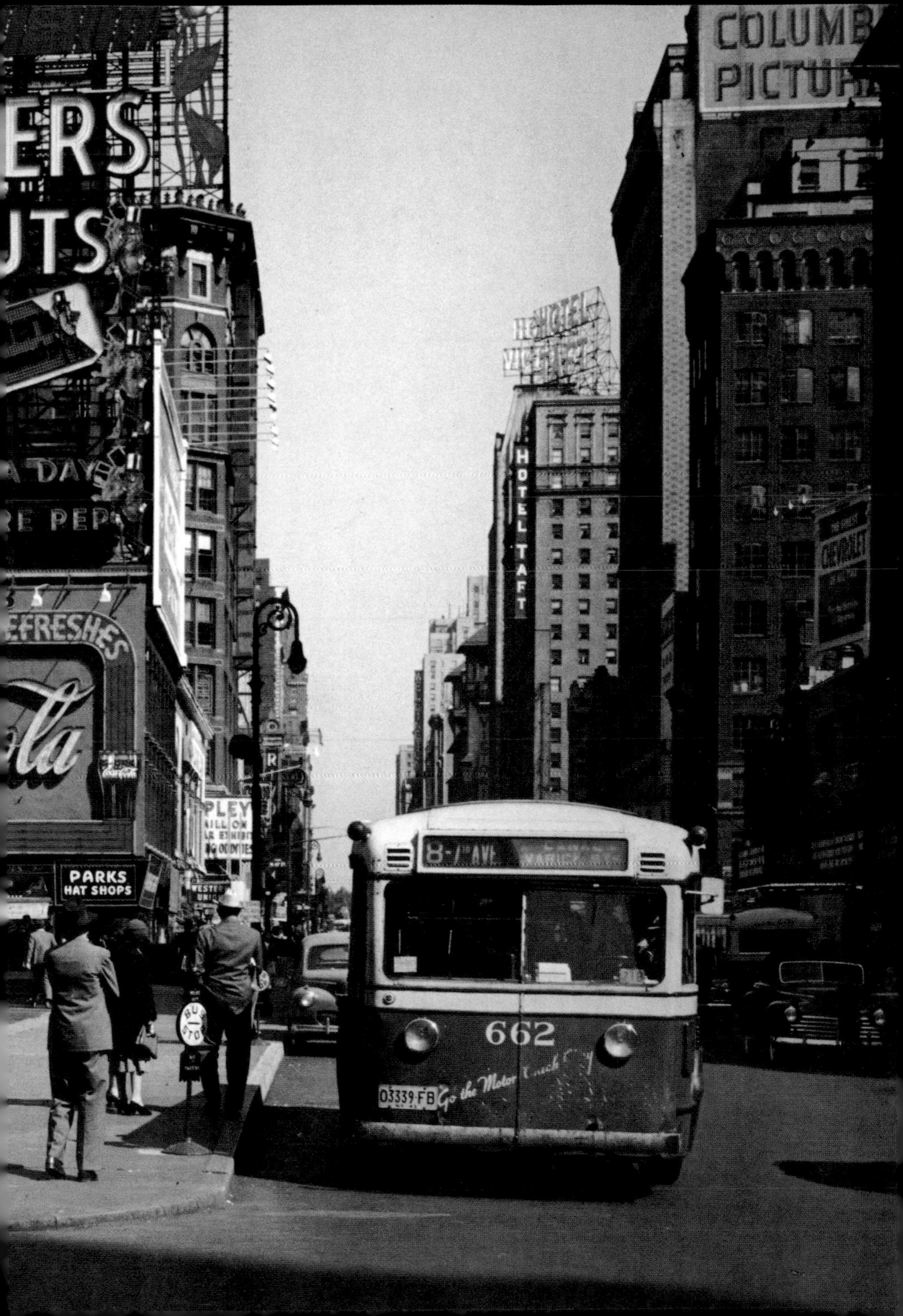
HOTEL TAFT
PARKS
HAT SHOPS
662

SURANCE COMPAN
NEW YORK
ESTABLISHED 1850
MON FONG WO CO.
MON FON

FAMOUS
BILL ROBI
COTT
50 SEPIAN STAR
DINNER
$1.50
COTTON
CLUB
Thelma Shop
FROCKS GOWNS

10/11 Symbol of the city: the Statue of Liberty at dusk in 1961. *Le symbole de la ville : la statue de la Liberté au crépuscule en 1961.* Das Symbol der Stadt: Die Freiheitsstatue in der Abenddämmerung, 1961.

12/13 Building boom: the skyscrapers around the Chrysler Building in the early 1960s. *Boom de la construction : les gratte-ciel autour du Chrysler Building, au début des années 1960.* Bauboom: Die Wolkenkratzer rund um das Chrysler Building, zu Beginn der 1960er-Jahre.

14/15 Neo-classicistic style: the facade of Pennsylvania Station in the early 1950s. *Style néoclassique : la façade de la Pennsylvania Station, au début des années 1950.* Im neo-klassizistischen Stil: Die Fassade der Pennsylvania Station, Anfang der 1950er-Jahre.

16/17 Business traffic: rush-hour on the streets of Downtown Manhattan. *Circulation intense : heure de pointe dans les rues de Downtown Manhattan.* Berufsverkehr: Rush-hour in den Straßen von Downtown Manhattan.

18/19 Palace of books: the New York Public Library photographed in the 1920s. *Le palais du livre : la New York Public Library, photographiée dans les années 1920.* Der Palast der Bücher: Die New York Public Library, fotografiert in den 1920er-Jahren.

20/21 Images become movies: the Strand Cinema on Broadway. *Les débuts du cinéma : le Strand Cinema à Broadway.* Wo die Bilder laufen lernten: Das Strand Cinema am Broadway.

22/23 Reach for the skies: the Chrysler Building in the 1930s, seen from 1st Avenue. *Haut dans le ciel : le Chrysler Building dans les années 1930, vu de la 1st Avenue.* Blick in den Himmel: Das Chrysler Building in den 1930er-Jahren, von der 1st Avenue her gesehen.

24/25 Good morning, New York: advertising in the window of the Manhattan Cafeteria around 1935. *Good Morning, New York : publicité en vitrine de la Manhattan Cafeteria vers 1935.* Good morning, New York: Werbung im Schaufenster der Manhattan Cafeteria um 1935.

26/27 Facades with fire-escapes: on a street on the Lower East Side of Manhattan. *Façades avec escaliers de secours : une rue du Lower East Side de Manhattan.* Fassaden mit Feuertreppen: In einer Straße auf der Lower East Side von Manhattan.

28/29 Splendour: the Grand Opera House (8th Avenue / 23rd Street) in 1936. *Strass et paillettes : le Grand Opera House (8th Avenue / 23rd Street) en 1936.* Glanz und Glamour: Das Grand Opera House (8th Avenue / 23rd Street) im Jahr 1936.

30/31 Black-and-white yet glittering: Times Square in 1938. *Arène de lumière en noir et blanc : le Times Square en 1938.* Die Glitzermeile in Schwarz-Weiß: Der Times Square anno 1938.

32/33 Hovering: an elevated railway against the backdrop of the Manhattan skyline. *Planer au-dessus des choses : un métro aérien devant le panorama de Manhattan Skyline.* Über den Dingen schweben: Eine Hochbahn vor der Kulisse von Manhattans Skyline.

34/35 Peanuts and Coca Cola: ads on Times Square in the early 1940s. *Peanuts et Coca Cola : panneaux publicitaires à Times Square, début des années 1940.* Peanuts und Coca Cola: Werbetafeln am Times Square, Anfang der 1940er-Jahre.

36/37 Before the big show: the entrance to Madison Square Garden. *Avant le grand spectacle : l'entrée du Madison Square Garden.* Vor dem großen Auftritt: Der Eingang zum Madison Square Garden.

38/39 Where East meets West: Chinatown in the mid-1940s. *Where East meets West : Chinatown, au milieu des années 1940.* Where East meets West: In Chinatown, Mitte der 1940er-Jahre.

40/41 Iron and steel: the Queensboro Bridge seen from 57th Street and Sutton Place. *Fer et acier : le Queensboro Bridge, vu de la 57th Street et de Sutton Place.* Eisen und Stahl: Die Queensboro Bridge, von der 57th Street und dem Sutton Place aus gesehen.

42/43 Bathed in light: the opening of Grand Central Station. *Bain de lumière : la Grand Central Station lors de son inauguration.* In Licht getaucht: Die Grand Central Station bei ihrer Einweihung.

44/45 Just Jazz: the Cotton Club before a concert starring Cab Calloway and Bill Robinson in 1932. *Just jazz : le Cotton Club avant un concert de Cab Calloway et Bill Robinson en 1932.* Just Jazz: Der Cotton Club vor einem Konzert mit Cab Calloway und Bill Robinson, 1932.

46/47 Apartments so far as the eye can see: a residential street in the Bronx in the 1950s. *Des appartements à perte de vue : une rue résidentielle dans le Bronx des années 1950.* Apartments so weit das Auge reicht: Eine Wohnstraße in der Bronx der 1950er-Jahre.

48/49 A new dynamism: the facade of the Guggenheim Museum on 5th Avenue in 1968. *Nouvel élan : la façade du Guggenheim Museum dans la 5th Avenue en 1968.* Neuer Schwung: Die Fassade des Guggenheim-Museums an der 5th Avenue, 1968.

50/51 Happy Birthday: Times Square on its 100th birthday (7 April 2004). *Happy Birthday : Times Square fête son centenaire (le 4 avril 2004).* Happy Birthday: Der Times Square an seinem 100. Geburtstag (7. April 2004).

52/53 At dusk: a water tower turned private parlour. *Au crépuscule : un château d'eau, transformé en salon privé.* Im Abendlicht: Ein Wasserturm, verwandelt in einen privaten Salon.

54/55 Manhattan by day: view over the famous skyscrapers. *Manhattan by day : des célèbres gratte-ciel vus du dessus .* Manhattan by day: Der Blick über die berühmten Wolkenkratzer.

56/57 Manhattan by night: New York, the glittering metropolis. *Manhattan by night : New York, métropole scintillante.* Manhattan by night: New York als Glitzer-Metropole.

"…The walls were lined with stuffed bookshelves, and more books were piled in leaning towers all over the room…"

Siri Hustvedt, in *The Blindfold*

«…Les murs étaient couverts d'étagères débordant de livres et d'autres ouvrages étaient empilés partout dans la pièce en tours penchées…»

Siri Hustvedt, dans *Les yeux bondés*

»…Die Wände waren mit überquellenden Bücherregalen zugestellt, und weitere Bücher stapelten sich überall im Raum zu schiefen Türmen…«

Siri Hustvedt, in *Die unsichtbare Frau*

INTERIORS

Intérieurs   Einsichten

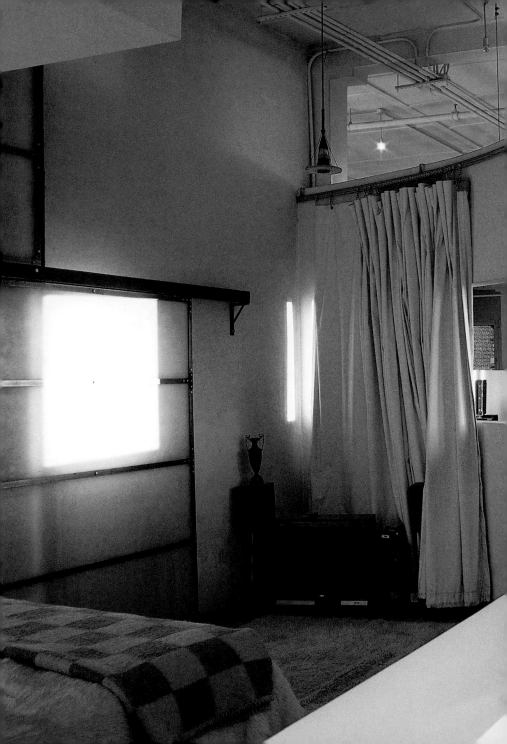

64/65 Postcard-panorama: view from a penthouse at Sutton Place. *Panorama de carte postale : la vue d'une penthouse à Sutton Place.* Postkarten-Panorama: Der Blick aus einem Penthouse am Sutton Place.

66/67 A white embrace: oversized living-room couch. *Décor immaculé : un gigantesque canapé.* Wohnlandschaft in Weiß: Überdimensionale Couch.

68/69 A florid touch: in a clearly designed kitchen. *Accueil fleuri : une cuisine au design épuré.* Blumengruß: In einer klar designten Küche.

70/71 In black-and-white: a bedroom in Manhattan. *Dormir en noir et blanc : un refuge en plein Manhattan.* Schlafen in Schwarz-Weiß: Ein Refugium mitten in Manhattan.

72/73 Room in red: an Asian-style retreat. *Room in red : un refuge aux accents asiatiques.* Room in Red: Pop Art angehauchter Rückzugsort.

74/75 Homage to Helmut Newton: a splendid coffee-table book. *Hommage à Helmut Newton : un magnifique ouvrage grand format.* Hommage an Helmut Newton: Ein prachtvoller Coffeetable-Band.

76/77 Behind the screens: in Hang Feng's apartment. *Derrière les coulisses : dans l'appartement de Hang Feng.* Hinter den Kulissen: In der Wohnung von Hang Feng.

78/79 Light and airy: delicate fabrics in Hang Feng's apartment. *Légers et vaporeux : des voiles délicats dans l'appartement de Hang Feng.* Leicht und luftig: Zarte Stoffe in der Wohnung von Hang Feng.

80/81 Fashion design with a view: Hang
Feng's Manhattan studio. *Créations de mode
avec vue sur Manhattan : chez Hang Feng.*
Modedesign mit Blick auf Manhattan: Bei Hang
Feng.

82/83 A touch of yellow: a lamp in Hang
Feng's bedroom. *Un accent jaune : lampe
dans la chambre à coucher de Hang Feng.*
Gelber Akzent: Lampe in Hang Fengs Schlafzimmer.

84/85 Salon style: chandelier and armchairs
in a SoHo apartment. *Style salon : lustre et
fauteuils dans un appartement de SoHo.* Im
Salon-Stil: Leuchter und Sessel in einer Wohnung in SoHo.

86/87 Highly polished: a long table for long
evenings. *Reluisante : table longue puur de
longues soirées.* Auf Hochglanz poliert: Eine
lange Tafel für lange Abende.

88/89 Floor-to-ceiling art: creative living in
SoHo. *De l'art du sol au plafond : ambiance
créative à SoHo.* Kunst vom Boden bis zur
Decke: Kreatives Ambiente in SoHo.

90/91 Focal point: dining table for relaxing
evenings with Eric Michelson. *Au cœur de la
pièce : la table pour des soirées détendues
chez Eric Michelson.* Im Mittelpunkt: Esstisch
für entspannte Abende bei Eric Michelson.

92/93 Pleasurable cooking area: at Eric
Michelson's apartment. *Cuisiner et apprécier :
chez Eric Michelson.* Kochen und genießen
zugleich: Bei Eric Michelson.

94/95 View of Manhattan: from the windows
of Eric Michelson's loft. *Enfilade de fenêtres :
vue dégagée sur Manhattan du loft d'Eric
Michelson.* Fensterfront: Freier Blick über Manhattan, von Eric Michelsons Loft aus gesehen.

96/97 Spacious: Eric Michelson's loft in Manhattan. *Trés vaste : le loft d'Eric Michelson à Manhattan.* Raum und Weite: Im Loft von Eric Michelson in Manhattan.

98/99 A place of honour: a painting in Sully Bonnelly's apartment. *Une place d'honneur : un tableau sur canapé dans l'appartement de Sully Bonnelly.* Ein Ehrenplatz: Weich gebettetes Gemälde in Sully Bonnellys Wohnung.

100/101 Different views: in the home of Sully Bonnelly. *Bien en vue : chez Sully Bonnelly.* Aus- und Ansichten: Bei Sully Bonnelly.

102/103 Books and artworks: in Sully Bonnelly's library. *Dans la bibliothèque : lecture et œuvres d'art chez Sully Bonnelly.* In der Bibliothek: Lesestoff und Kunstwerke bei Sully Bonnelly.

104/105 Relaxing after his travels: Sully Bonnelly's living room. *Détente après de nombreux voyages : le salon de Sully Bonnelly.* Refugium nach vielen Reisen: Das Wohnzimmer von Sully Bonnelly.

106/107 Twin chairs: designer furniture at Sully Bonnelly's. *Chaises jumelles : meubles design chez Sully Bonnely.* Zwillingsstühle: Designermöbel bei Sully Bonnelly.

108/109 A place in the sun: Gigi Sharp and George Gilpin's terrace in East Village. *Une place au soleil : la terrasse de Gigi Sharp et George Gilpin à East Village.* Ein Platz an der Sonne: Auf der Terrasse von Gigi Sharp und George Gilpin im East Village.

110/111 Creative touch: Gigi Sharp and George Gilpin's loft. *Touche créatrice personnelle : le loft de Gigi Sharp et George Gilpin.* Kreativer persönlicher Touch: Im Loft von Gigi Sharp und George Gilpin.

112/113 A dash of color: view into Gigi Sharp and George Gilpin's kitchenette. *Touches de couleur : la kitchenette de Gigi Sharp et George Gilpin.* Farblich abgesetzt: Blick zur Kitchenette von Gigi Sharp und George Gilpin.

114/115 Eye-catchers: furniture and accessories at the home of Gigi Sharp and George Gilpin. *Captent l'attention : meubles et accessoires chez Gigi Sharp et George Gilpin.* Eyecatcher: Möbel und Accessoires bei Gigi Sharp und George Gilpin.

116/117 Typical New York: the Midtown loft of writer Amy and editor Frank. *Typiquement new-yorkais : le loft Midtown de l'écrivain Amy et de l'éditeur Frank.* Typisch New York: Das Midtown-Loft von Schriftstellerin Amy und Herausgeber Frank.

118/119 Mickey Mouse meets music: Amy and Frank's bedroom. *Mickey Mouse meets music : dans la chambre à coucher d'Amy et de Frank.* Mickey Maus meets music: Im Schlafzimmer von Amy und Frank.

120/121 Open spaces: Amy and Frank's spacious kitchen. *Espaces ouverts : cuisine spacieuse d'Amy et de Frank.* Offene Räume: In der weitläufigen Küche von Amy und Frank.

122/123 Velvety blue: soft sofas in Amy and Frank's loft. *Velours bleu : canapés moelleux dans le loft d'Amy et de Frank.* Samtblau: Weiche Sofas im Loft von Amy und Frank.

124/125 Colour and form: 1970s style at Dr. Mark Rabiner's in Gramercy Park. *Formes et couleurs : le style des années 1970 chez le Dr. Mark Rabiner à Gramercy Park.* Form und Farbe: Der Stil der 1970er bei Dr. Mark Rabiner im Gramercy Park.

126/127 Gazing into the past: at the home of Dr. Mark Rabiner. *Retour sur le passé : chez le Dr. Mark Rabiner.* Wie ein Blick in die Vergangenheit: Bei Dr. Mark Rabiner.

"... a few children's toys scattered on the floor – a red truck, a brown bear, a green space monster ..."

Paul Auster, in *City of Glass*

«...Quelques jouets étaient éparpillés sur le sol, – un camion rouge, un ours brun, un monstre vert de l'espace...»

Paul Auster, dans *Trilogie new-yorkaise*

»...Einige Spielsachen waren über den Boden verstreut – ein roter Lkw, ein brauner Bär, ein grünes Ungeheuer aus dem Weltraum...«

Paul Auster, in *Die New York-Trilogie*

DETAILS

Details Détails

THE FATE OF THE
Immodest Blonde
(PUZZLE FOR PILGRIMS)

Patrick Quentin

Beauty and blood...
a marriage feast for
MURDER!

COMPLETE AND
UNABRIDGED

The
PLUTONI
BLOND

He was the last P.I. on the planet, but
save the world from a nuclear-powered
exotic-dancing femb...

JOHN ZAKOUR &
LAWRENCE GANEM

omicide Blonde
A Harper Novel of Suspense
by Maurice Procter

883
The Case of the Nude Beauty's Corpse

Stone Cold Blonde

ADAM KNIGHT

A SIGNET BOOK
Complete and Unabr

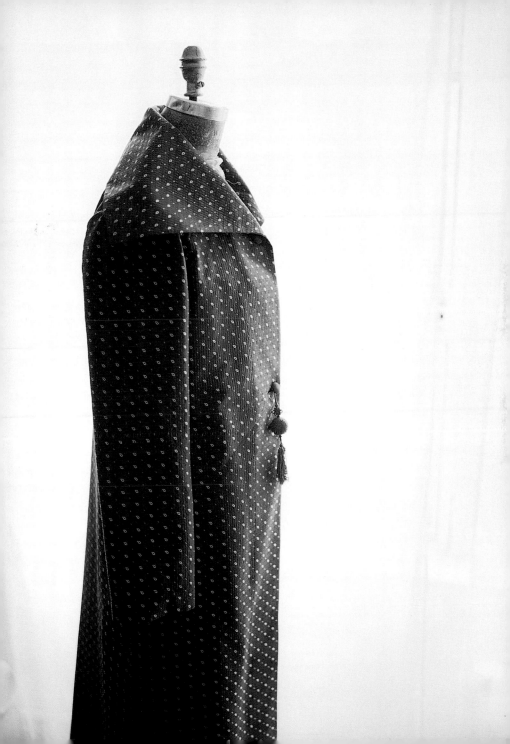

  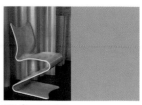

134 Crazy animals: seen from Gigi Sharp und George Gilpin's loft. *De drôles d'animaux : vu du loft de Gigi Sharp et George Gilpin.* Tolle Tiere: Blick aus dem Loft von Gigi Sharp und George Gilpin.

136 Stacked: cast-off drawers at Amy and Frank's place. *Entassés : des tiroirs au rencart chez Amy et Frank.* Gestapelt: Ausrangierte Schubladen bei Amy und Frank.

137 Time in abundance: Gigi Sharp and George Gilpin's clocks. *Du temps à revendre : chez Gigi Sharp et George Gilpin.* Zeit im Überfluss: Bei Gigi Sharp und George Gilpin.

138 Of a piece: chair in Gigi Sharp and George Gilpin's loft. *En un seul jet : chaise dans loft de Gigi Sharp et George Gilpin.* Wie aus einem Guss: Stuhl im Loft von Gigi Sharp und George Gilpin.

140 Hallucinatory effect: in Gigi Sharp and George Gilpin's loft. *Illusion optique : dans le loft de Gigi Sharp et George Gilpin.* Sinnestäuschung: Im Loft von Gigi Sharp und George Gilpin.

141 Tea for two: at Gigi Sharp and George Gilpin's dining table. *Teatime en bleu : à la table de Gigi Sharp et George Gilpin.* Blaue (Tee)-Stunde: Am Esstisch von Gigi Sharp und George Gilpin.

142 Safe landing: model airplane on Amy and Frank's wall. *Atterrissage forcé : maquette d'avion en décor mural chez Amy et Frank* Sicher gelandet: Modellflugzeug als Wandschmuck bei Amy und Frank.

144 Striking: couch-table at Amy and Frank's. *Belle plastique : table de salon chez Amy et Frank.* Schön plastisch: Couchtisch bei Amy und Frank.

145 Propped up: a studio in SoHo. *Échelonnées : toiles dans un atelier de SoHo* Gestaffelt: In einem Atelier in SoHo.

146 Entrance / Exit: lettering on the wall of the bedroom. *Entrée et sortie : lettres sur le mur de la chambre à coucher.* Hinein und hinaus: Buchstaben an der Schlafzimmerwand.

148 A shrine in Manhattan: at the home of Charlie Green. *Un temple à Manhattan : vu chez Charlie Green.* Ein Schrein in Manhattan: Bei Charlie Green.

149 Perfectly arranged: ceramics on Sully Bonnelly's wall. *Agencée de manière exemplaire : la poterie chez Sully Bonnelly.* Mustergültig angeordnet: Keramik bei Sully Bonnelly.

150 Full agenda: in Sully Bonnelly's apartment. *Agenda bien rempli : dans l'appartement de Sully Bonnelly.* Überquellender Terminkalender: In der Wohnung von Sully Bonnelly.

152 Pretty bags: in Hang Feng's apartment. *Jolis saces : dans l'appartement de Hang Feng.* Hübsche Beutel: In der Wohnung von Hang Feng.

153 Taking a closer look: magnifying glass and books. *Pour y voir de plus près : loupe et livres.* Sehen Sie genau hin: Lupe und Bücher.

155 About blondes: Charlie Green's favourite reading matter. *Bien blonde : la littérature préférée de Charlie Green.* Ganz schön blond: Charlie Greens Lieblingsliteratur.

156 A comfortable spot: Sully Bonnelly's favourite chair. *Un coin douillet : le fauteuil préféré de Sully Bonnelly.* Lieblingsplatz: Plüschsessel bei Sully Bonnelly.

157 Light art: in Amy and Frank's Midtown loft. *Art du luminaire : loft Midtown d'Amy et Frank.* Licht-Kunst: Im Midtown-Loft von Amy und Frank.

158 Timely: unique clocks owned by Gigi Sharp and George Gilpin. *Il est temps : tic-tac de pièces uniques chez Gigi Sharp et George Gilpin.* Es ist an der Zeit: Tickende Unikate bei Gigi Sharp und George Gilpin.

160 Well guarded: shelves in Amy and Frank's apartment. *Bien gardées : étagères chez Amy et Frank.* Gut bewacht: Regale bei Amy und Frank.

161 Guitar within reach: in Amy and Frank's apartment. *Guitare à portée de main : dans l'appartement d'Amy et de Frank.* Griff zur Gitarre: In der Wohnung von Amy und Frank.

163 White porcelain: on Gigi Sharp and George Gilpin's shelves. *Porcelaine blanche : sur les étagères de Gigi Sharp et George Gilpin.* Weißes Porzellan: In den Regalen von Gigi Sharp und George Gilpin.

164 At the ready: Dr. Mark Rabiner's dumb-bells. *Prêt pour l'entraînement : les haltères du Dr. Mark Rabiner.* Bereit zum Training: Dr. Mark Rabiners Hanteln.

166 On three legs: side table in Dr. Mark Rabiner's apartment. *Sur trois pieds : table basse dans le studio du Dr. Mark Rabiner.* Auf drei Beinen: Beistelltisch im Apartment von Dr. Mark Rabiner.

167 One-eyed and glowing: an orange cat sculpture in Dr. Mark Rabiner's apartment. *Borgne et orange fluo : chat sculpté chez le Dr. Mark Rabiner.* Einäugig und leuchtend orange: Katzenskulptur bei Dr. Mark Rabiner.

169 Like in a cinema: at Dr. Mark Rabiner's home. *Comme au cinéma : chez le Dr. Mark Rabiner.* Ein Ausblick wie im Kino: Bei Dr. Mark Rabiner.

170 Pretty in pink: a new shade of bathroom. *Pretty in pink : de nouveaux tons dans la salle de bains.* Pretty in Pink: Ganz neue Töne im Bad.

171 Like on stage: in a penthouse at Sutton Place. *Comme sur scène : dans une penthouse à Sutton Place.* Wie auf einer Bühne: In einem Penthouse am Sutton Place.

172 Blooming: silk roses in a Manhattan apartment. *Épanouies : des roses en soie dans un studio de Manhattan.* Aufgeblüht: Seidenrosen in einem Apartment mitten in Manhattan.

174 Kitsch is art: birds from the flea market and sparkling glass jewels. *Le kitsch est un art : oiseaux de brocante et bijoux de verre étincelants.* Kitsch ist Kunst: Vögel vom Flohmarkt und funkelnde Glasjuwelen.

175 Stripes: a bluish-yellow sequin jacket with a portrait of a dog. *Rayée : une veste à paillettes bleue et jaune avec un portrait de chien.* Im Streifenlook: Ein blaugelbes Pailettenjackett mit Hundeportrait.

176 America's ex-First Couple: plate showing the Johnsons. *Ex-couple présidentiel américain : assiette à l'effigie des Johnson.* Das Ex-First-Couple Amerikas: Teller mit einem Abbild der Johnsons.

178 Great things in store: Colette's overflowing wardrobe. *Le nec plus ultra : la penderie de Colette et ses trésors.* Fundus vom Feinsten: Der überquellende Kleiderschrank von Colette.

179 Standing to attention: a model designed by Hang Feng. *Le mannequin : un modèle de Hang Feng.* Modell stehen: Ein Entwurf von Hang Feng.

180 Up to the sky: the staircase at the home of Gigi Sharp and George Gilpin. *Grimpant vers le ciel : l'escalier chez Gigi Sharp et George Gilpin.* In Richtung Himmel: Das Treppenhaus von Gigi Sharp und George Gilpin.

183 Visual attraction: detail from Hang Feng's apartment. *Stimulant optique : un détail chez Hang Feng.* Optische Reize: Detail bei Hang Feng.

184 Watched by the cat: handbags at Hang Feng's apartment. *Bien gardés : sacs à main chez Hang Feng.* Mit Katzenaugen bewacht: Handtaschen bei Hang Feng.

185 Decorative: bust belonging to Hang Feng. *Paré d'un collier : un buste chez Hang Feng.* Schmuckvoll: Büste bei Hang Feng.

186 Taxi! The Yellow Cabs on the streets of New York. *Taxi! Les Yellow Cabs dans les rues de New York.* Taxi! Die Yellow Cabs auf den Straßen von New York.

Photo Credits

The Hotel Book.
Great Escapes South America
Ed. Angelika Taschen
Hardcover, 360 pp. / € 29.99 /
$ 39.99 / £ 24.99 / ¥ 5.900

The Hotel Book.
Great Escapes North America
Ed. Angelika Taschen
Hardcover, 400 pp. / € 29.99 /
$ 39.99 / £ 24.99 / ¥ 5.900

The Hotel Book.
Great Escapes Asia
Ed. Angelika Taschen
Hardcover, 400 pp. / € 29.99 /
$ 39.99 / £ 24.99 / ¥ 5.900

"This is one for the coffee table, providing more than enough material for a good drool. Gorgeousness between the cover." —*Time Out,* London, on *Great Escapes Africa*

"Buy them all and add some pleasure to your life."

60s Fashion
Ed. Jim Heimann

70s Fashion
Ed. Jim Heimann

African Style
Ed. Angelika Taschen

Alchemy & Mysticism
Alexander Roob

Architecture Now!
Ed. Philip Jodidio

Art Now
Eds. Burkhard Riemschneider,
Uta Grosenick

Atget's Paris
Ed. Hans Christian Adam

Bamboo Style
Ed. Angelika Taschen

Barcelona,
Restaurants & More
Ed. Angelika Taschen

Barcelona,
Shops & More
Ed. Angelika Taschen

Ingrid Bergman
Ed. Paul Duncan, Scott Eyman

Berlin Style
Ed. Angelika Taschen

Humphrey Bogart
Ed. Paul Duncan, James Ursini

Marlon Brando
Ed. Paul Duncan, F.X. Feeney

Brussels Style
Ed. Angelika Taschen

Cars of the 70s
Ed. Jim Heimann, Tony Thacker

Charlie Chaplin
Ed. Paul Duncan, David
Robinson

China Style
Ed. Angelika Taschen

Christmas
Ed. Jim Heimann, Steven Heller

James Dean
Ed. Paul Duncan, F.X. Feeney

Design Handbook
Charlotte & Peter Fiell

Design for the 21st Century
Eds. Charlotte & Peter Fiell

Design of the 20th Century
Eds. Charlotte & Peter Fiell

Devils
Gilles Néret

Marlene Dietrich
Ed. Paul Duncan, James Ursini

Robert Doisneau
Ed. Jean-Claude Gautrand

East German Design
Ralf Ulrich/Photos: Ernst Hedler

Clint Eastwood
Ed. Paul Duncan, Douglas
Keesey

Egypt Style
Ed. Angelika Taschen

Encyclopaedia Anatomica
Ed. Museo La Specola Florence

M.C. Escher

Fashion
Ed. The Kyoto Costume Institute

Fashion Now!
Eds. Terry Jones, Susie Rushton

Fruit
Ed. George Brookshaw,
Uta Pellgrü-Gagel

Greta Garbo
Ed. Paul Duncan, David
Robinson

HR Giger
HR Giger

Grand Tour
Harry Seidler

Cary Grant
Ed. Paul Duncan, F.X. Feeney

Graphic Design
Eds. Charlotte & Peter Fiell

Greece Style
Ed. Angelika Taschen

Halloween
Ed. Jim Heimann, Steven Heller

Havana Style
Ed. Angelika Taschen

Audrey Hepburn
Ed. Paul Duncan, F.X. Feeney

Katharine Hepburn
Ed. Paul Duncan, Alain Silver

Homo Art
Gilles Néret

Hot Rods
Ed. Coco Shinomiya, Tony
Thacker

Grace Kelly
Ed. Paul Duncan, Glenn Hopp

London, Restaurants & More
Ed. Angelika Taschen

London, Shops & More
Ed. Angelika Taschen

London Style
Ed. Angelika Taschen

Marx Brothers
Ed. Paul Duncan, Douglas
Keesey

Steve McQueen
Ed. Paul Duncan, Alain Silver

Mexico Style
Ed. Angelika Taschen

Miami Style
Ed. Angelika Taschen

Minimal Style
Ed. Angelika Taschen

Marilyn Monroe
Ed. Paul Duncan, F.X. Feeney

Morocco Style
Ed. Angelika Taschen

New York Style
Ed. Angelika Taschen

Paris Style
Ed. Angelika Taschen

Penguin
Frans Lanting

Pierre et Gilles
Eric Troncy

Provence Style
Ed. Angelika Taschen

Safari Style
Ed. Angelika Taschen

Seaside Style
Ed. Angelika Taschen

Signs
Ed. Julius Wiedeman

South African Style
Ed. Angelika Taschen

Starck
Philippe Starck

Surfing
Ed. Jim Heimann

Sweden Style
Ed. Angelika Taschen

Tattoos
Ed. Henk Schiffmacher

Tokyo Style
Ed. Angelika Taschen

Tuscany Style
Ed. Angelika Taschen

Valentines
Ed. Jim Heimann, Steven Heller

Web Design:
Best Studios
Ed. Julius Wiedemann

Web Design:
Best Studios 2
Ed. Julius Wiedemann

Web Design:
E-Commerce
Ed. Julius Wiedemann

Web Design: Flash Sites
Ed. Julius Wiedemann

Web Design:
Music Sites
Ed. Julius Wiedemann

Web Design: Portfolios
Ed. Julius Wiedemann

Orson Welles
Ed. Paul Duncan, F.X. Feeney

Women Artists
in the 20th and 21st Century
Ed. Uta Grosenick